THE HUBBLE
TELESCOPE LAUNCH

BY KATE MIKOLEY

Gareth Stevens
PUBLISHING

Cataloging-in-Publication Data

Names: Mikoley, Kate.
Title: The Hubble Telescope launch / Kate Mikoley.
Description: New York : Gareth Stevens Publishing, 2019. | Series: History just before you were born | Includes glossary and index.
Identifiers: ISBN 9781538231388 (pbk.) | ISBN 9781538230275 (library bound) | ISBN 9781538233184 (6 pack)
Subjects: LCSH: Hubble Space Telescope (Spacecraft)--Juvenile literature. | Space telescopes--Juvenile literature. | Outer space--Exploration--Juvenile literature.
Classification: LCC QB500.268 M54 2019 | DDC 522.2919--dc23

First Edition

Published in 2019 by
Gareth Stevens Publishing
111 East 14th Street, Suite 349
New York, NY 10003

Copyright © 2019 Gareth Stevens Publishing

Designer: Sarah Liddell
Editor: Therese Shea

Photo credits: Cover, p. 1 Frank Whitney/The Image Bank/Getty Images; newspaper text background used throughout EddieCloud/Shutterstock.com; newspaper shape used throughout AVS-Images/Shutterstock.com; newspaper texture used throughout Here/Shutterstock.com; halftone texture used throughout xpixel/Shutterstock.com; p. 5 (Galileo) Hulton Archive/Stringer/Hulton Archive/Getty Images; p. 5 (Hubble) UniversalImagesGroup/Contributor/Universal Images Group/Getty Images; p. 7 Photo 12/Contributor/Universal Images Group/Getty Images; p. 9 NASA/Contributor/The LIFE Picture Collection/Getty Images; p. 10 Historical/Contributor/Corbis Historical/Getty Images; p. 11 NASA/Handout/Hulton Archive/Getty Images; p. 13 (*Challenger*) High Contrast/Wikimedia Commons; p. 13 (icicles) BotMultichillT/Wikimedia Commons; p. 15 Torquemada082/Wikimedia Commons; p. 17 (main) Flugaal/Wikimedia Commons; p. 17 (inset) Science & Society Picture Library/Contributor/SSPL/Getty Images; p. 19 Crisco 1492/Wikimedia Commons; p. 20 Tryphon/Wikimedia Commons; p. 21 Mayhaymate/Wikimedia Commons; pp. 23, 24 TheDJ/Wikimedia Commons; p. 25 Ras67/Wikimedia Commons; p. 27 JIM WATSON/Staff/AFP/Getty Images.

CONTENTS

Words in the glossary appear in **bold** type
the first time they are used in the text.

GALILEO'S TELESCOPES

In 1609, Italian philosopher and mathematician Galileo Galilei heard about an instrument that could help people see faraway things as if they were nearby. He was quickly able to come up with improvements to the tool, which we call a telescope. Soon Galileo was creating increasingly powerful telescopes and using them to make observations about the night sky. He discovered moons around Jupiter and stars that can't be seen with the naked eye.

In the centuries that have passed since Galileo's time, even more advances have been made in telescopes. Today, telescopes range from small devices you can set up in your home to enormous **observatories** used by scientists to study the universe. The most famous telescope—the Hubble Space Telescope—is used in space!

MORE TO THE STORY

While there have been many great telescopes before it, the Hubble Space Telescope is the first major optical telescope to go to space. An optical telescope gathers and magnifies visible light.

EDWIN HUBBLE

GALILEO GALILEI

BEFORE TELESCOPES, EVERYTHING PEOPLE KNEW ABOUT THE UNIVERSE CAME FROM WHAT COULD BE SEEN WITH THE NAKED EYE.

WHO'S HUBBLE?

The Hubble Space Telescope is named after Edwin Hubble, an astronomer whose discoveries changed our understanding of the universe. After serving as a soldier in World War I (1914–1918), Hubble began working at the Mount Wilson Observatory in California. There, he used the largest and most powerful telescope of the time for his research. He discovered evidence that the universe extends past our **galaxy**, the Milky Way, and that galaxies exist beyond our own.

WHY OBSERVE FROM SPACE?

Telescopes on the ground can tell us quite a bit about the universe, but not everything. Celestial bodies are natural objects outside of Earth's atmosphere, such as planets or stars. The layers of gas that make up the atmosphere obscure, or make it hard to see, certain celestial bodies by absorbing or **distorting** rays of light coming from them. That's why observations from ground-based telescopes may not be completely clear and often don't show as much detail.

Scientists knew a telescope placed in space would greatly improve their understanding of the galaxy and the universe beyond. A space telescope, above Earth's atmosphere, would receive much sharper, brighter, and more detailed images. This idea became a reality through the hard work of some brilliant scientists.

MORE TO THE STORY

Earth's atmosphere distorts light from stars. That's why stars appear to twinkle!

A REFLECTING TELESCOPE

There are two main kinds of telescopes: refracting and reflecting. Refracting telescopes use lenses to bend light. Reflecting telescopes use mirrors to reflect light. The Hubble Space Telescope is a reflecting telescope. Its mirrors reflect light from celestial objects into cameras and spectrographs. Spectrographs divide light into different colors, which allows scientists to study the makeup of space objects. No one looks through the Hubble with their eyes. Instead, radio waves send the Hubble's data to Earth.

EXPLODING STAR

THE HUBBLE SPACE TELESCOPE'S CAMERAS HAVE CAPTURED PICTURES OF PLANETS, STARS, AND EVEN GALAXIES IN SPACE!

THE LST PROJECT

The idea of putting a telescope in space first received attention in 1923. German scientist Hermann Oberth suggested a rocket could launch a telescope into orbit around Earth. More than 20 years later, a scientist named Lyman Spitzer Jr. wrote about the benefits of having a telescope in space. For years, Spitzer worked to get support from other scientists to put a large telescope into orbit.

Finally, in 1969, the National Academy of Sciences approved what was then called the Large Space Telescope (LST) project. In July 1969, Neil Armstrong became the first man to walk on the moon. Though this was celebrated as a "giant leap for mankind," space exploration began to lose funding. Without financial support, the LST project was in trouble.

MORE TO THE STORY

After the 1969 moon landing, many people began to lose interest in exploring space. The National Aeronautics and Space Administration (NASA) lost funding, and the LST's budget shrank.

WHEN ASTRONAUTS BUZZ ALDRIN (SHOWN HERE) AND NEIL ARMSTRONG WALKED ON THE MOON, MANY PEOPLE CONSIDERED THE "SPACE RACE" BETWEEN THE SOVIET UNION AND THE UNITED STATES TO BE OVER.

FORMING NASA

In 1957, the Soviet Union launched Sputnik I, its **satellite** that would orbit Earth. The new development sparked a "space race" between the Soviet Union and the United States. In 1958, the United States successfully launched the satellite Explorer I. Later that same year, the US government established NASA. This was the beginning of the organization that would eventually launch the Large Space Telescope.

People didn't give up completely on exploring space, though. NASA and the groups it worked with decided to build a space shuttle. This craft could go to space, orbit Earth, and eventually return to the ground safely. The space shuttle could be used more than once for multiple missions. It could also be used to get the Large Space Telescope into space.

The people working on the LST project wanted to make sure the telescope would last for many years. Many of its parts were made to be replaceable. In addition to getting the telescope into space, the space shuttle could be used to bring it back to Earth for repairs—or bring people to space to do the repairs!

MORE TO THE STORY

In 1977, US Congress approved the funding for the LST. That year, the LST was renamed the "Hubble Space Telescope" in honor of Edwin Hubble.

THE ESA ENTERS THE PROJECT

In 1975, the European Space Agency (ESA) joined NASA on the LST project. They contributed 15 percent of the LST's funding by adding a special camera—the Faint Object Camera—and other important parts. In return, NASA agreed that ESA scientists could use the telescope to observe space at least 15 percent of its operating time. From then on, the ESA and NASA worked together on the project.

IN 1981, THE SPACE SHUTTLE *COLUMBIA* LAUNCHED. IT WAS THE FIRST REUSABLE SPACECRAFT. SCIENTISTS HOPED A CRAFT LIKE THIS COULD SOON CARRY THE SPACE TELESCOPE.

DISASTER STRIKES

With funding finally in place, construction of the telescope began. Though the Hubble's launch was planned for 1983, building it took longer than expected—and cost more money than first estimated. Experts working on the project faced many challenges, but worked hard to come up with the best design. They remodeled certain parts to make sure they operated as well as possible within the limits of funding. By 1985, the telescope was finally finished and set to launch in the fall of 1986.

However, in January 1986, the space shuttle *Challenger* exploded shortly after launching. This **disaster** stunned the world. Space shuttle flights stopped for 2 years while the cause was investigated—and the telescope couldn't launch without a shuttle.

MORE TO THE STORY

During the time the shuttle program was on hold, engineers improved the telescope's **solar panels**, computers, and communications systems.

ICICLES ON THE LAUNCH TOWER

FLORIDA EXPERIENCED UNUSUALLY COLD WEATHER ON THE NIGHT BEFORE THE *CHALLENGER* LAUNCH, WHICH IS BELIEVED TO HAVE LED TO THE DISASTER.

THE *CHALLENGER* DISASTER

On January 28, 1986, tragedy struck the US space program. The shuttle *Challenger* launched from Cape Canaveral, Florida, with seven astronauts on board. Just 73 seconds after liftoff, the *Challenger* exploded, killing the entire crew. The shuttle program—and the Hubble launch—was immediately put on hold. NASA studied the explosion and found that the cold weather leading up to the launch reduced the strength of some shuttle parts and led to the accident.

THE LONG-AWAITED LAUNCH

While the shuttle program was on hold, the telescope went through more testing, and its finished parts were stored, waiting until the final product was cleared to launch. In 1988, the space shuttle *Discovery* took off on NASA's first space shuttle mission since the *Challenger* accident. Two years later, on April 24, 1990, *Discovery* launched for its tenth time. On this mission, it was finally carrying the Hubble Space Telescope into space!

Discovery's crew flew the Hubble 373 miles (600 km) above Earth. This was a record altitude for a space shuttle. On April 25, *Discovery*'s robotic arm placed the telescope into orbit. After more than 20 years since the LST project was approved, the Hubble Space Telescope was ready to explore the unknown.

MORE TO THE STORY

The launch of the Hubble Space Telescope was considered the biggest advancement in astronomy since Galileo's telescope!

HUBBLE, WE HAVE A PROBLEM

Soon after the Hubble was positioned in orbit, it became clear there was a problem. While the pictures it sent back were much sharper than those taken by telescopes on the ground, they still weren't as clear as they were supposed to be. It turned out there was a slight flaw in a mirror that made it the wrong shape. This flaw was enough to reduce image quality. Luckily, scientists fixed this problem on the first Hubble servicing mission in 1993.

THIS IMAGE SHOWS THE HUBBLE SPACE TELESCOPE BEING PLACED INTO ORBIT ON APRIL 25, 1990.

HUBBLE STATS

The Hubble Space Telescope is very different from a telescope you might use at home. For one thing, it's much larger. At 43.5 feet (13.3 m) long, it's about the same length as a school bus. It weighs as much, too. When it first launched, it weighed around 24,000 pounds (10,886 kg). However, after servicing missions, it now weighs nearly 27,000 pounds (12,247 kg).

The Hubble moves around 17,000 miles (27,359 km) per hour, or about 5 miles (8 km) per second. That means it orbits Earth about once every 95 minutes. The telescope runs on energy from the sun. It has two solar panels that change the sun's light into electrical energy. The energy can be stored so the telescope works even when it's not getting much sunlight.

MORE TO THE STORY

The Hubble can detect objects that are 10 billion times more faint than anyone could see with their naked eyes!

THE HUBBLE SPACE TELESCOPE MOVES SO FAST IT COULD TRAVEL FROM ONE SIDE OF THE UNITED STATES TO THE OTHER IN JUST 10 MINUTES.

HOW THE MIRRORS WORK

The Hubble has a primary, or main, mirror nearly 8 feet (2.4 m) in **diameter**. The mirror's size aids it in collecting a great amount of light. The light that hits it gets reflected into a secondary mirror that's much smaller than the primary mirror—only 1 foot (0.3 m) in diameter. The smaller mirror reflects the light back through a hole in the primary mirror. From there, the light travels to the cameras and spectrographs.

HUBBLE'S ACHIEVEMENTS

Since the Hubble Space Telescope began its mission in 1990, it's made more than 1.3 million observations, providing the world with amazing views that we would never have been able to see otherwise. It has helped scientists make discoveries about our solar system and given us a deeper understanding about the creation of celestial bodies.

Before the Hubble Space Telescope, astronomers knew a star forms when clouds of gas and dust collapse due to the force of gravity. The matter at the center of this mass becomes a hot core that grows into a star. However, astronomers couldn't see all parts of a star's formation. In 1995, the Hubble took the first pictures of the star-forming process in an area of our galaxy called the Orion Nebula. It has also captured images of dying stars.

MORE TO THE STORY

One of the Hubble's many discoveries was the existence of moons around Pluto.

THE HUBBLE CAPTURED THIS IMAGE OF THE PILLARS OF CREATION, A REGION WHERE STARS ARE ACTIVELY FORMED. THE PILLARS OF CREATION ARE LOCATED IN A CLUSTER OF STARS CALLED THE EAGLE NEBULA.

MORE TO EXPLORE

The Hubble Space Telescope opened our eyes to parts of the universe previously unknown. However, even now, there's so much that we still don't know—and so much more to explore. Scientists are learning with every image the Hubble takes. Even the things we currently think we know about space, comets, planets, stars, galaxies, and the universe as a whole could change in the future as **technology** becomes more advanced.

Edwin Hubble also gave his name to an idea called the Hubble constant. This is the rate at which the universe is expanding—and an important part of estimating how old the universe is. Hubble first tried to measure this value in 1929.

Over the years, technology has allowed us to make more precise measurements. Up until the Hubble Space Telescope launch, experts estimated the age of the universe to be anywhere from 10 billion to 20 billion years. By using the Hubble Space Telescope to observe certain kinds of stars in other galaxies, scientists calculated the first **accurate** rate of the universe's expansion. They used it to determine that the universe is nearly 14 billion years old!

IMAGE OF A DISTANT GALAXY CAPTURED BY THE HUBBLE SPACE TELESCOPE

MORE TO THE STORY

Dark matter is invisible to light so the Hubble can't capture an image of it. Scientists have not yet observed dark matter, but know it exists because it has an effect on galaxies.

INVISIBLE UNIVERSE

The Hubble Space Telescope helped scientists discover a mysterious force called dark energy. While still mysterious to even the most knowledgeable experts, we do know dark energy causes the expansion of the universe to speed up. By using the Hubble Space Telescope, scientists have been able to guess that dark energy makes up about 68 percent of the universe. Another 27 percent is invisible "dark matter." That means only about 5 percent of the universe can be seen!

THE HUBBLE HAS TAKEN IMAGES SHOWING THE FARTHEST SEEN DEPTHS OF THE UNIVERSE. DATA FROM THE TELESCOPE'S FINDINGS HAS BEEN USED IN MORE THAN 15,000 SCIENTIFIC PAPERS!

SERVICING MISSIONS

Unlike other spacecraft, such as the International Space Station and the space shuttles, the Hubble Space Telescope orbits Earth without people inside. However, over the years, astronauts have visited it to do repairs and make sure everything is running smoothly. Regular service insures that the telescope can keep working like it's supposed to. In fact, service is part of the reason it has operated as long as it has.

So far, there have been five servicing missions to the Hubble Space Telescope, the first of which was in 1993 when the primary mirror was repaired. Several other new instruments were also added during this servicing mission. In 1997, even more instruments were added, and older parts of the telescope that were no longer usable were exchanged with newer components.

MORE TO THE STORY

On the 1997 servicing mission, astronauts added a tool to the Hubble Space Telescope that could observe infrared light. This is light that produces rays longer than red light. Infrared light can't be seen.

ASTRONAUTS TRAVELED IN A SPACE SHUTTLE TO REACH THE HUBBLE SPACE TELESCOPE AND PERFORM NECESSARY REPAIRS AND SERVICE.

WALKING IN SPACE

Whenever an astronaut leaves a craft in space, they perform a "spacewalk." Spacewalks are a necessary part of servicing the Hubble Space Telescope. During the first servicing mission in 1993, the crew of the space shuttle *Endeavor* spent more than a week in orbit and set a record for performing spacewalks 5 days in a row. One of the crew members, Jeffrey Hoffman, later said this first mission was the "most **complex** shuttle mission that had ever been undertaken."

The next servicing mission took place in 1999. The repairs during this assignment focused on the gyroscopes, also simply called gyros. Gyros are a key part of the Hubble Space Telescope. They're used to measure the rate of the telescope's motion as it moves. They make sure it's pointing correctly. In order for the telescope to work, it must have three gyros operating together. A total of six are kept on board, with three used as backups in case the others fail.

One gyro failed in 1997, a second in 1998, and a third in 1999. When a fourth gyro failed in late 1999, the Hubble was temporarily unable to operate. Luckily, the repair crew was able to replace all six gyroscopes and get the telescope back into action.

1999 SERVICING MISSION

MORE TO THE STORY

In the near future, NASA will decide whether to let the Hubble Space Telescope deorbit and fall to Earth or push it into a higher orbit.

HUBBLE'S LAST SERVICING

The fifth and final servicing mission of the Hubble Space Telescope was in 2009. As usual, new instruments were added, but there was one different addition: a special part that will someday help remove the telescope from service. Though experts knew it would be some time until the Hubble was ready to retire, they added this device to the base of the telescope in preparation for its final days.

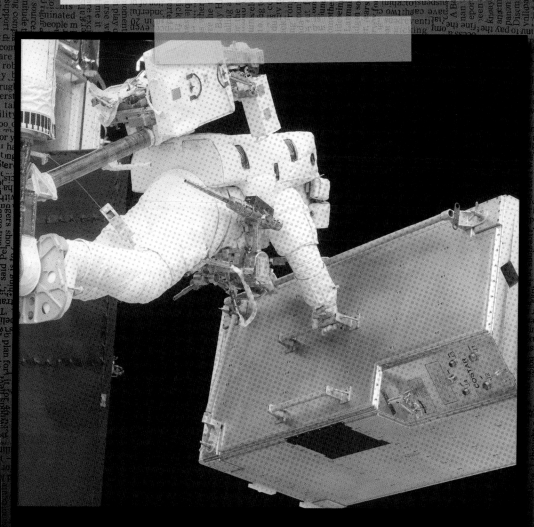

IN 2009, THE COSTAR DEVICE, WHICH HAD SOLVED THE HUBBLE'S MIRROR FLAW, WAS REMOVED. NEW TECHNOLOGY MEANT IT WAS NO LONGER NEEDED.

A CREW OF HUNDREDS

On the ground, hundreds of people work to make sure the Hubble Space Telescope is operating properly. The Hubble's control center is located at the Goddard Space Flight Center in Greenbelt, Maryland. There, engineers communicate with the telescope using special satellites. The telescope has antennae that are able to receive messages from these satellites. One of the Hubble's main computers handles commands that point the telescope, while the other collects data and sends it to the satellites so it can be transmitted to Earth.

The scientists at the Goddard Space Flight Center send the data to the Space Telescope Science Institute in Baltimore. The information is translated into scientific units that can be used by researchers. Astronomers all over the world study the information.

MORE TO THE STORY

Very few people actually get to use the Hubble Space Telescope, but anyone can view a collection of images taken by the telescope that are available to the public.

OVER 30 ASTRONAUTS HAVE FLOWN TO THE HUBBLE
SPACE TELESCOPE, BUT HUNDREDS MORE PEOPLE ON THE
GROUND HAVE BEEN RESPONSIBLE FOR ITS OPERATION.
THOUSANDS HAVE USED ITS DATA.

A UNIQUE COMPETITION

Anyone can ask to use the Hubble Space Telescope. However, very few of
these requests are accepted. Each year, people submit proposals to the
Space Telescope Science Institute to use the telescope. Anyone can apply,
but the competition is tough. Scientists all over the world want the chance
to study the universe through the Hubble. Around 1,000 applications are
received each year, but only about 200 are chosen.

WHAT'S NEXT?

The Hubble Space Telescope was originally intended to operate for about 15 years, but it's been running for much longer than that! Today, NASA is working on plans for a new telescope. The James Webb Space Telescope will be even larger than the Hubble, with a main mirror about 21.3 feet (6.5 m) in diameter. The other major difference is that the Webb telescope will orbit the sun, almost 1 million miles (1.6 million km) away from Earth. Scientists hope it will be able to look even deeper into the universe than the Hubble.

Still, no one's planning on getting rid of the Hubble Space Telescope just yet. Experts are hopeful the two remarkable telescopes can operate together for a time, shedding more light on the universe's many mysteries.

MORE TO THE STORY

The James Webb Space Telescope is scheduled to launch in 2020. Experts think it will be able to help them learn what the universe looked like after the **Big Bang**!

WHO WAS JAMES WEBB?

James Webb, the man the new telescope is named for, oversaw NASA from 1961 to 1968. During this time, the Apollo program was born, which resulted in the first moonwalk in 1969. When announcing the name of the telescope, former NASA official Sean O'Keefe said that Webb "took our nation on its first voyages of exploration, turning our imagination into reality. Indeed, he laid the foundations at NASA for one of the most successful periods of astronomical discovery."

THE JOURNEY OF THE HUBBLE SPACE TELESCOPE

1920s: EDWIN HUBBLE DISCOVERS GALAXIES BEYOND THE MILKY WAY USING THE TELESCOPE AT THE MOUNT WILSON OBSERVATORY.

1923: SCIENTIST HERMANN OBERTH PROPOSED A TELESCOPE COULD BE PUT INTO ORBIT AROUND EARTH.

1958: NASA IS ESTABLISHED.

1969: THE LARGE SPACE TELESCOPE (LST) PROJECT IS APPROVED.

1975: THE EUROPEAN SPACE AGENCY JOINS NASA ON THE LST PROJECT.

1977: CONGRESS APPROVES FUNDING FOR THE LST. THE TELESCOPE IS NAMED FOR EDWIN HUBBLE.

1986: THE HUBBLE SPACE TELESCOPE IS SCHEDULED TO LAUNCH, BUT THE *CHALLENGER* DISASTER PUTS IT ON HOLD.

1990: THE CREW OF THE SPACE SHUTTLE *DISCOVERY* PUTS THE HUBBLE SPACE TELESCOPE INTO ORBIT.

1993: THE HUBBLE'S PRIMARY MIRROR IS REPAIRED AS PART OF THE FIRST SERVICING MISSION.

1997: ASTRONAUTS ADD A TOOL TO THE HUBBLE SPACE TELESCOPE THAT AIDS IT IN OBSERVING INFRARED LIGHT.

1999: THE HUBBLE'S GYROS ARE REPLACED IN THE TELESCOPE'S THIRD SERVICING MISSION.

2002: ASTRONAUTS REPLACE THE HUBBLE'S SOLAR PANELS AND INSTALL A CAMERA THAT DOUBLES ITS FIELD OF VIEW.

2009: ASTRONAUTS TRAVEL TO THE HUBBLE FOR ITS FIFTH AND FINAL SERVICING MISSION.

GLOSSARY

accurate: free from mistakes

Big Bang: a huge explosion that scientists believe caused the beginning of the universe

complex: having to do with something with many parts that work together

diameter: the distance from one side of a round object to another through its center

disaster: an event that causes much suffering or loss

distort: to twist out of a natural, normal, or original shape or condition

galaxy: a large group of stars, planets, gas, and dust that form a unit within the universe

observatory: a place used for the scientific observation of heavenly bodies

satellite: an object that circles Earth in order to collect and send information or aid in communication

solar panel: a group of solar cells forming a flat surface on a spacecraft that use the sun's light to create electricity

technology: tools, machines, or ways to do things that use the latest discoveries to fix problems or meet needs

FOR MORE INFORMATION

BOOKS

Hamilton, John. *Hubble Space Telescope: Photographing the Universe.* Minneapolis, MN: Abdo Publishing, 2018.

Hutchison, Patricia. *Exploring Beyond Our Solar System.* Mankato, MN: The Child's World, 2016.

Morey, Allan. *The Hubble Space Telescope.* Minneapolis, MN: Bellwether Media, 2018.

WEBSITES

About the Hubble Space Telescope
www.nasa.gov/mission_pages/hubble/story/index.html
Read about the Hubble Space Telescope on NASA's website.

Awesome 8 Hubble Space Telescope
kids.nationalgeographic.com/explore/
awesome-8-hub/hubble-space-telescope/
Check out eight of the coolest images the Hubble Space Telescope has ever taken.

Repairing Hubble
airandspace.si.edu/stories/editorial/repairing-hubble
Read more about how Hubble has been repaired and check out some photos here.

INDEX